Abiding in Christ

staying with God in a Busy World

James Keating, Ph.D.

The Institute for Priestly Formation

IPF Publications

THE INSTITUTE FOR PRIESTLY FORMATION
IPF Publications
2500 California Plaza
Omaha, Nebraska 68178-0415
www.IPFPublications.com

Printed in the United States of America
ISBN-13: 978-0-9981164-6-4

Cover design by Timothy D. Boatright
Vistra Communications
Tampa, Florida

THE INSTITUTE FOR PRIESTLY FORMATION

MISSION STATEMENT

The Institute for Priestly Formation was founded to assist bishops in the spiritual formation of diocesan seminarians and priests in the Roman Catholic Church. The Institute responds to the need to foster spiritual formation as the integrating and governing principle of all aspects for priestly formation. Inspired by the biblical-evangelical spirituality of Ignatius Loyola, this spiritual formation has as its goal the cultivation of a deep interior communion with Christ; from such communion, the priest shares in Christ's own pastoral charity. In carrying out its mission, the Institute directly serves diocesan seminarians and priests as well as those who are responsible for diocesan priestly formation.

THE INSTITUTE FOR PRIESTLY FORMATION
Creighton University
2500 California Plaza
Omaha, Nebraska 68178-0415
www.priestlyformation.org
ipf@creighton.edu

ABIDING IN CHRIST: STAYING WITH GOD IN A BUSY WORLD

You walk into the house after work and what awaits you may be a family "emergency": unwanted bills, a sick child, broken pipes, teenage angst, or more! Life comes at you fast, but your heart craves inner peace, some stable routine in daily life or quiet time with your spouse. Instead, what you know is hurried commitments, unexpected drama, and a daily life that carries more stress than desired.

Yet, within our hearts, we have a source of peace. It is not easily discovered in the rush of self-imposed events or work mandated by others. Within us is a peace "that surpasses all understanding" (Phil 4:7), a peace given by the One who has dwelled there since our Baptism, God Himself. By noting this inner peace, am I not mocking our demanding schedules, our necessary busy-ness? Perhaps I do not understand the many commitments you hold, what they take from you, or reduce you to. In fact, I am inviting you to that peace precisely because I take those many commitments seriously and experience, along with you, *a persistent longing* for the "simple life."

That longing is God offering just that—a simpler life. Unfortunately, our lives are often defined by the rush of the day and not by God's offer of intimacy. We feel trapped by the obligations that descend upon us, and this may lead us to resent or resist the truth that we are "blessed." Life is complex. This complexity is due mostly to sin, ignorance, and self-involvement. Gazing at the lives of the saints shows us another reality: lives filled with activity and initiative, but with an enviable quality . . . diminished anxiety and stress. The peace that possesses the saints makes its power known within their bodies, bodies that rest in prayer. This prayer is not a "technique" used to reduce heart rate, as many meditation movements promote today. An interior life is not "useful" in the sense that physical exercise is. Instead, prayer's benefits are *fundamental*, *substantial*, and *fulfilling to* our *very humanity*, rather than simply beneficial to our physical health or emotional equilibrium. No, prayer is more than useful. It is a way of being in communion that *defines* our very lives.

We may object: "I am *not* a saint! I have four kids and hold two jobs to feed and house them—don't pander to me with your poetry about resting in prayer." Even if our feelings do not precisely mirror this reaction, we can see what fuels it: emotional pain born of *desire*. A person may feel that "I *want* to rest in prayer. I *want* to receive peace from God. I *want* to be a saint, but I *can't*. I am too busy, too sinful, too ordinary, or too distracted to ever achieve any such thing."

Our faith can show us that those frustrated longings for peace need *not* be. In fact, we can use such longings to orient our lives. Before we believe this, however, we need to recognize two vital truths. First, the spiritual life—a life of holiness, prayer, and moral living—is not an achievement but is, rather, a gift. Second, the very frustrated desires you notice in yourself are what Christ wants to fulfill in you *more than you can even imagine*! Human happiness—our deepest desire—is not simply for the "holy ones"; it is the inheritance of all the baptized in grace. We simply have to claim it. We claim it through the way of renunciation and through the way of celebration. In so doing, we "have life and have it more abundantly" (Jn 10:10).

In both the way of renunciation and the way of celebration, Christ is doing most of the "work." Remember that this life of longings fulfilled is mostly a gift to us, not a chore pursued through sheer willpower. Suffering is involved in becoming interiorly peaceful, but it is a suffering of letting things go rather than a chore of taking up tasks.

The Way of Renunciation

What is the way of renunciation? As we become aware that Christ wants to give Himself—and end the isolation we feel due to the demands of life—we come to know Him living in our hearts. We want to live within Christ and have Him live within us. We want to abide with Him in the normal routine of our day; but just as we find it difficult to deepen our human relationships, we find it difficult to abide with God. As with our human relationships, we must consider one vital question: What is preventing this friendship with God from going deeper? In our human relationships, many things prevent us from deepening friendships, such as time constraints, personality traits, disparate interests, or geographic distance. With Christ, the only barrier is sin.[1] To remove this barrier and open up the joy of holy communion with Him is why He came as Savior. It is not simply the rush of daily life that robs us of inner peace; the primary thief is sin. Compounding the force of sin is our error in thinking that the spiritual life, the life of our soul, is not as real as our bodies. Over time, it would help us to receive a deep peace if we acknowledged that our choices affect not only our bodies, but also our relationship with God, who is spirit.

I remember once being tempted to buy some doughnuts. As the temptation filled me, I immediately thought about the effect eating doughnuts would have on my body and chose an apple instead. Such reasoning does not always come so easily in my relationship with God. Because I think my body is more "real" than my relationship with God, I have often sinned. With more ease and less reflection than I give to resisting unwanted calories, I risk destroying communion with Him when I sin. We must pray to end our erroneous thinking that the body is more real than the soul, or that the soul and body are somehow not one! If we can do this, renouncing sin will come with greater ease.

How, then, do we renounce sin? How do we deplete its power over our emotional life? How can I reduce my attraction toward "the evil I do not want" (Rom 7:19)? These questions reveal great emotional pain around our favorite sinful temptations. God labors to gift us with a healing of these emotions and restore the dignity that is ours as followers of Christ. Receiving such healing is more about receiving *God's love* than suffering the pain of saying, "No," to our favorite sins. Right in the midst of temptation's struggle, God invites us to open our hearts to be loved. We struggle with sin because we want to stay in our "own place" (Acts 1:25). We *do not* want His love; we want the sin that is attracting us. Since the Fall, we are wired to respond to the distraction that is sin. Habitually behaving out of our communion with God is undermined when our wounded senses react to the sparkling foil that temptation uses to catch our eye. Such strange opposition—choosing sin instead of what we really want (God)—is the very condition that causes humanity to cry out for a savior. Executing sin, in all its forms, leaves us weak, truly in need of the healing salve of the One who is Christ.

To rise above our own self-will is difficult; and very often, we prefer the empty life of selfishness to the full life Christ offers. This full life is ours for the living *if* we would only turn away from sin and toward Him. Attempting to turn from sin on our own, however, is precisely what makes conversion so difficult. Doing it "on our own" is a recipe for giving up on conversion. The key to remaining somewhat stable in our conversions is to turn toward Him *in our sin*, not after we have achieved an illusory self-mastery. Sin will never be conquered by our willing it so; it will only be tempered, healed, and seen as offensive as a result of our remaining with Christ.

The more we place ourselves in the presence of His love—most especially through prayer, Eucharistic adoration, *Lectio Divina* (the prayerful reading of Scripture), service to the poor, and worship at Sunday Eucharist—the *more our affection for sin will recede.*

How do we begin to participate in the abundant living Christ promises? We do so by placing ourselves in His presence. That is all—we just start there. Over time, our desire to be in *His presence* will transform into a deeper desire to remain in *communion* with Him sacramentally. In this communion, God, who is beauty itself, will reorient our desires, flatten our interest in sin, and reveal sin for what it truly is: boring and empty. God is the opposite of such boredom. He is life itself, beauty itself, and goodness itself. Being vulnerable to His love brings us a dynamic interior life, releasing peace and joy. He brings us to a real change, to a point where we *no longer* want to choose our favorite sins; but instead, we want to choose the real and full life He offers.

What do we renounce when we want to be healed of our attraction to sin? We renounce our consistent drift toward ego independence. We do this by making the positive choice to be with God in prayer. The suffering that is our conversion is not our "hard work" against sin, per se. Rather, it is our vigilance against choices to "hide" from God or "go to our own place." Instead, we need to *remain in His presence and abide with Him.*

We also need to be humble about any victory over our new disinterest in sin. The history of the saints tells us that temptations can return as a storm. If they do (and we should not be surprised if, and when, they do), we exist in a new place of trust with Jesus. We need only turn our will to Him again, be with Him, and seek His forgiveness in prayer and in the Sacrament of Reconciliation. The latter is most crucial because it, along with regular participation at Holy Mass and reception of the Eucharist, is the dynamo of divine power that continues to heal our affection for sin. Let us renounce self-will and the idea of saving ourselves by our own ethical code, and instead stand always in His presence in our need, be vulnerable to His love, and *receive our conversion* and with it, the very reason Christians worship in joy.

The Way of Celebration

What does it mean to celebrate? Originally, it carried a sense of glorification or even worship. By remaining in Christ's presence, we notice our disordered desires progressively recede. The space formerly occupied by sinful interests becomes filled with joy and gratitude. This is where we want to live from now on, in that space of joy and gratitude. Joy is not a personality trait like "cheerfulness." It is a *deep current of peace* that causes us to be grateful and humble. Any accidental traits of "cheery" joy actually come from *this deep well* of gratitude and humility. In fact, joyful people are attractive to us because we seek to draw from that same well of humble gratitude.

Christ knew, of course, that we would want to thank Him when we began to notice our waning interest in sin. Knowing human nature to its core, He knew we needed to thank Him not once, in a cursory gesture of kindness, but in *a sustained way*. Experiencing a healing from sin by Christ is so profound that life itself becomes a way of *thanksgiving*. Only a life of patterned thanksgiving and celebration is proportionate to the gift Christ gave us on the Cross and in the Resurrection. On the night He died, He provided for this proportionate response and gave the Church Holy Orders and the Eucharist.

We do not just say "thank you" for salvation; we participate again and again in the love from which it springs. Such relational and progressive participation is necessary for we who are in time. Until conversion is permanently established within us in Heaven, we need time to mature into our reception of Divine Love. With each celebration of the Eucharist, we progressively enter the life He opened for us: which is to share in the love among the Father, Son, and Holy Spirit. We enter His love for us gradually, internalizing it over time until such love defines us. The pattern of renunciation and celebration is our way to sanctity, our way of internalizing His love for us.

Thus, the Catholic life involves tasting the dregs of boredom in sin, choosing to be with Christ in prayer so He may heal our interest in sin, and celebrating His power to heal by regularly receiving His love within the Eucharist.

Growing Interior Peace

As we follow the way of renunciation and celebration, we will find the interior peace we deeply crave as it takes up residence within our hearts. Even as our days remain busy with many activities, we can still "abide with Him,"—first, in our growing love of prayer and renunciation of sin, and second, in our deepening love for the life we receive from the Eucharist, a life of thanksgiving.

To remain with Him, we need to develop one further habit of love: hospitality toward His coming in love *throughout the day*. Of course, we need to go to the Blessed Sacrament to pray, but we also need to learn how to receive His love during the course

of a workday or family commitments. To receive
His love, we need to be affectively vulnerable toward
Him and become adept at noticing when He is shar-
ing His love in ordinary circumstances. Such vulner-
ability or openness toward God is built within us. To
be open is to *want* God's love and presence to affect
us, move us, change us in some way. It is a conscious
decision to remain in God's presence and welcome
the influence that such a presence has upon our
thinking, our choices, and our feelings.

How Do We Maintain Our Availability?

Married couples will oftentimes fill their work-
places with photos or reminders of their spouse,
so they can emotionally connect with each other
throughout the day—even if only for a short
moment—by glancing at these icons. The heart in
love *wants* to stay connected with the one it loves.
God loves us, so He also wishes to initiate an affective and intellectual connection with us. This initia-
tion by God *becomes prayer* if we respond in faith,
hope, and love,[2] regardless of where we are in our
daily commitments.

Each day, we are busy with many challenges, but
it is still possible to receive Christ's love in the midst
of them. Unfortunately, daily events often rob us of

the sense of His presence. If we are not vigilant, the daily grind mistakenly communicates that ordinary life is spiritually lifeless; our days are simply filled with the agendas of others and ourselves. Daily life can begin to feel enclosed, airless, and self-absorbed. Over time, we can lose a sense of transcendence. Losing a sense of the spiritual is similar to being in a marriage that loses its erotic energy. When spouses become defined by work, success, or some other duty that economic need presses upon them, they can lose touch with one another. The most human-izing of realities—intimate communion with the one we love—becomes undermined by the clamoring of economic and familial demands vying for immediate attention. God, too, can be lost in such a tumult.

Also threatening our intimate communion with God and those we love are the unattended emotional wounds within us; those neurotic promptings that bid us to protect, promote, and over-analyze our-selves. Like the attention we give to achievement and work, our lives become stuffy and airless, filled only with the self. Addressing such emotional wounds with therapy can help us become free to donate ourselves to God and our vocation. Such therapy is sought in the Eucharist, spiritual direction, psycho-logical counseling, serving others, and in obediently responding to the (sometimes subtle) invitations of our spouse, children, friends, and God to "Come spend time with me. Just come and be with me."

Within the suffocating realities of self-absorption and economic busy-ness is a subtle invitation from God to come and rest with Him. As we progressively fill our hearts with His presence through a life of celebration and renunciation, our interior spiritual senses become more acute. We come to notice more quickly how He moves to console us, thereby counteracting our grief, or how He identifies a damaging lie that we believe about Him, ourselves, and others. We come to see, in other words, that we are never alone. This is vital because our perception of loneliness, or the reality of prolonged loneliness, is an ignition to sin and despair. God wishes to heal the loneliness at the core of our wounded human nature. To heal in this way is why He came to live among us in Jesus, and why Jesus formed a community around Him—so that we might see, despite the weight of sin, that reality is a communion of love. Near the opening of Genesis, we see God's attitude toward loneliness: "It is not good for the man to be alone" (Gn 2:18). Coming to sense His presence enfolded within our ordinary days refutes the condition and lie of loneliness that Satan wishes to exploit.

Our hearts and minds can be cluttered with streams of thoughts and images that have very little connection to our present concerns or work. Frequently, either consciously or unconsciously, we are very busy with the continuous flow of content that runs through our minds, seemingly on autopilot. Among all these "pictures" and "voices," God wishes to speak to us. He longs to sound a voice of love or an invitation to conversion.

How can we better listen *to* Him and *for* Him amid this interior jumble? First, we can cultivate the habit of interior silence. Interior silence is a character trait that *makes room* for a voice beyond our own. It is hospitality deep within the soul that renders us available for visits from God. Ironically, interior silence is cultivated by committing ourselves to periods of *external* silence throughout the day. Intentionally seeking a silent environment gives birth to interior silence. From this place of interior silence, we can more easily live in communion with God, which fulfills the very purpose of His indwelling. "The same [Holy] Spirit who moves and motivates God in his actions is now also in us and impels us to live in the same way as God."[3] Interior silence cultivates a state of diminished interference between our heart and the Trinity and prepares us to receive and remain in communion with God. In marriage, silence is the necessary prerequisite to a kiss. One cannot kiss or be kissed by a talking spouse! By giving silence a key position in our spiritual lives, we create an environment conducive to abiding with the Trinity. Silence creates the condition for the possibility of a Divine kiss. "The spirituality of St. Bernard's conception of the mystic kiss of Christ . . . signifies nothing else than to receive the inpouring of the Holy Spirit. . . . [t]his gift conveys both the light of knowledge and the unction of piety."[4] In other words, as we enter into and begin to love our times of silence, we are invited to call upon the Holy Spirit to abide with us there. God cannot "kiss" us if we are doing all the talking. Silence facilitates God's holy communion with us.

We want to receive this "inpouring" by way of our interior hospitality. Our silence communicates an attitude of total availability to God's love. The work of the Holy Spirit is to bind us to Christ and, thus, to the Father; the Spirit *is* Holy Communion. He seeks us out in the ordinary circumstances of our day to assure us that Heaven is not far away—it is coming to us from within the ordinary. We only need to *notice* His presence moving our affections from within. His voice speaks gently to us, confirming that

15

Heaven is not "up there." Heaven entered human existence with the coming of Christ and is now a stable presence in the Sacraments and within us by the indwelling Spirit. If only we come to discern His presence lodged within the crowd of feelings and thoughts that inhabit us, we will know daily life as saturated with God. Thus, silence is the essential medium for prayerful union with the Trinity. Having an interior silence can provoke a change of heart because silence is not emptiness but rather, conveys a promised and anticipated union—a union fostered by the activity of listening and desire. Silence filled with listening and eager desire reaches its crescendo in an act of self-gift, a quiet handing over of oneself to Jesus. Silence is not the absence of words but the fullness of presence, a presence ordered toward gift.

Our present popular culture is afraid of silence. It senses that within prayerful silence lies the very destruction of its own superficial, relentless, and noisy emptiness. The popular culture keeps yelling louder, not realizing that what noise offers is only momentary and without substance. The Divine Presence fills our hearts, confidently voicing His love in calm and consistent tones. God has no need to shout, as He is not passing away like the current insecure "age" (Rom 12:2).[5]

God Moving within Us

God will help us pray in a *silent room*, within a *silent heart*, and also in the midst of a noisy city or venue because He awakens our desire to cradle silence *within us*. We can be assured that He will give us the grace to love silence because it facilitates our capacity to receive His love. God's usual way of communicating through prayer is from within our deepest affections. From within, He assures us that there is hope, that we are not alone, and that we are good and do not disappoint Him. From within our affections, He reminds us that we are capable of resisting temptation and choosing new behaviors. He shares Himself with us when we love and express goodness toward others and when we resolve to pray. When we refuse to love or pray, He encourages us from within to start again. God communicates Himself to us *in our struggle* to receive all His graces. He wants to share in our journey to holiness. We want to push against any negative stream of thought that crowds our minds and hearts. We want to begin each day in praise, adoration, and thanksgiving, thereby clearing a space in our hearts for His coming. In many ways, God is like the little child who bounds into his parents' bedroom early in the morning; joyful, smiling, and yearning to be with them.

By listening for His movements within our hearts, we come to host Him more securely. We want to internalize His presence, to welcome and guard it as we begin our day. "And I will ask the Father, and he will give you another Advocate to be with you always, the Spirit of truth, which the world cannot accept, because it neither sees nor knows it. But you know it, because *it remains with you*, and *will be in you. I will not leave you orphans; I will come to you*" (Jn 14:16-18, emphasis mine). Our God is a God who comes *to us*—do we sense Him doing so?

God's Voice

From the images, words, and affections that reside within us, God communicates what is true. As we receive communication from Him, our faith, hope, and love deepen. Both reason and affect combine to define what the Church calls the heart. From within minds influenced by love (our heart), the indwelling Spirit both speaks to and guides us.[6]

Perceiving God is never a matter of merely reason *or* affect; it is always a matter of using our whole selves to discern God's Word. Our r*easoning* mind is *affected* by both what is true and who we love. We have to learn to listen to and for Him. He will sound different than the normal stream of noise spilling in from popular culture. His voice brings an invitation to "have life and have it more abundantly" (Jn 10:10). His voice always sounds like both consolation and challenge. The consolation is aimed at alleviating our real burdens, and the challenge invites us to live with Him and not simply in "this age" (Rom 12:1-2). His voice awakens us to our true dignity and is always delivered to us in peaceful confidence, never extreme in tone or emotion. It has to be this kind of voice. God is self-possessed, and nothing influences Him except His own loving nature. Most of our lives should be spent trying to learn ways of listening only to His voice in our heart. Of course, it is crucial to seek guidance from a spiritual director and pastor in order to discern if we are really hearing God or simply hearing our unhealed thoughts and emotions. "The heart is the place of decision, deeper than our psychic drives. It is the place of truth, where we choose life or death. It is the place of encounter, because as image of God we live in relation: it is the place of covenant."[7]

Learning to listen to and follow such a heart is to live a simple life. Our lives are complex because we disobey our hearts. We keep thinking that disobeying what is true will somehow give us more, when, in fact, there is no *more* than the truth. To live in the truth is to live in reality. For the Catholic, reality is to live within the beauty and limits of our vocation. Our sacramental vocations—Baptism, Matrimony, Holy Orders—are given to us as ways of participating in reality. That is why Christ invited us into our vocations and sustains us in them through the Eucharist, Reconciliation, and the service that each vocation demands. To be baptized, confirmed, and perhaps married, are the ways we participate in all that is His—that is, His life, His mysteries of love, and His actions that reveal His identity and purposes. To look beyond our vocation is to overreach and court being tempted by fantasy (i.e., some form of infidelity to our vocations). When we choose fantasy instead of reality, we leave the simple life and enter the very definition of complexity.

Since the popular, political, and economic cultures have *imperceptibly* (and sometimes deceptively) formed our consciences, we now have to *intentionally* form them anew. This is founded upon our relationship to Christ in the Church. Pondering the loving action of Christ in the Eucharist and listening to Him in the Scriptures, the lives of the saints, and the content of the *Catechism* are sure sources of formation. These sources lead to inner peace, simplicity of life, and creative generosity toward others. If we recommit ourselves to walk these sure paths into Christ's own life, then our lives will stay simple, our consciences will be properly formed, and our behavior will mature over time to generous self-giving.

As I noted above, human happiness is more gift than task. Here is the crux of that gift: the more we *attend* to the mysteries of Christ in prayer, *participate* in them at the Eucharist, and *meditate* upon them in Scripture, the more our imaginations will brighten with Christian creativity and our wills will ignite in charitable behavior. From all this, we become happy, whole, integrated, simple, and holy. Attending, participating, and meditating are the attitudes whereby we express our availability to receive love from God, as well as surrender ourselves to Him. Love always includes both receptivity and self-donation; and it is self-revelation, the adhesive of all love, that secures this receptivity and self-donation. Anonymity is the very opposite of love; Christ *is* the deep desire of God to make Himself known. Christ, then, is the revelation of God's true intentions toward us: to invite, attract, and seduce[8] all into His "home" (Lk 14:23). He does this inviting through Christ's self-sacrifice upon the Cross and the unrelenting life that flows through the Resurrection. Even this momentous revelation does not affect immediate conversion in us; most change in us is progressive and developmental. God has the power to wait, influence, and suffer our conversions at levels of love we cannot even imagine.

We need patience as well. Sometimes, because our conversions are slow, we give up on the relationship; however, it is God's constitution *never* to give up on our relationship. Trust in that truth and return to Him often. God never counts how many times we stray. He only longs to welcome us back to His table for the feast of love.[9] To love God, then, is more His gift to us than our gift to Him. It is certainly a real, freely entered relationship that we have with God, or it would not be worth suffering. But His life and love, which is grace, always takes the initiative and sustains the communion. Such is the depth of His desire to be with us (Lk 14:17).[10]

Knowing that God searches for and wants to remain in communion with us ignites the leading edge of inner peace for which we are longing. Such a belief saves us from joining the error-prone quest for perfectionism, the quest to catch God's eye with our ethical achievements (i.e., "See how good I am; now, will you love me?"). There is nothing we can do to earn God's love. His gift of self and communion is freely given. It is already a "done deal" in and through His Son's journey of love on earth. If we simply position ourselves at the weak points of creation—those places where God's love flows freely, such as the sacramental life, our vocations fully lived, the Scriptures encountered as prayer, and the poor received in their pain—we will be taken up into a Holy Communion. God's love for us is a fact. The drama of our lives is clear: Do we love Him?

Five Practical Ways to Remain with God

1. Vocation

It is always good to receive our vocations anew. We can do this by sitting with God in a church, by offering prayer in the quiet of our home, or being someplace out in nature. To receive our vocation anew is to anchor our minds, bodies, and hearts in that way of life to which He calls us. That life, our vocation, is the one that makes it easiest for God to reach us. After all, He is the one who called us to be baptized, married, in holy orders, or in religious vows. He saw this way of life as the easiest way for us to become saints. We love our vocation—its beauty, its joys—and so, we can carry the crosses that come with it. The vocation itself is not our cross; that would simply be cruel. Rather, our vocation properly discerned and given to us by God *is our joy*. We should, therefore, marvel at our vocation and give Him thanks for caring so deeply as to fashion this particular life for us. As we raise our hearts in gratitude to Him for the vocation *itself,* our vocation etches more deeply upon our hearts and we receive all the particularities of it in new and vivid ways. This vocation is the basis of all our prayer life. It is the way we *live in reality*, and the way God reaches us most fully. Being so, we need to guard, celebrate, and receive our vocation completely as gift.

2. Prayer Time

Prayer is the hardest commitment of each day, until our "yeses" to prayer inhabit our hearts. It may take years of starting and stopping before prayer becomes the desire of our hearts. Mysteriously, for others, prayer is a committed delight from the start of their mature faith life. Either way, prayer is the center of all things because our dispositions and behaviors flow from our interior communion with Christ. Living in communion with God should be understood in the same way that a mature and holy married couple always consults with one another before making decisions. In this way, decisions become the occasion for deeper peace and unity. In executing the decision, the couple is one; and their bond of love is renewed as their unified actions go forth. So it is with those who have grown mature in prayer. They would never make a decision that weakens the bond between themselves and Christ. They go forward, in consultation with the Spirit, only enacting the vocational and weighty decisions that flow from vulnerable and honest prayer.

Such a way of living is a delight, not a burden. Prayer feels like a burden only when we are moving away from a life of fantasy, entertainment, and engagement with the superficial slogans and politics of popular culture. As these idols of immediate gratification recede and we heed the invitation to enter more deeply into relationship with the Trinity, we may feel a resistance to prayer precisely because it lacks immediate gratification in its character of sobriety, silence, and simplicity. The heart trained in immediate gratification will resist the sobriety of prayer and remain fascinated with the thousand diversions offered by the media; but the prayerful heart knows that such superficialities are useful only when relegated to their proper and limited use.

As we commit to a set time for prayer each day, the siren voices tempting us back to technological addiction will decrease in volume and, eventually, become easier to resist or ignore. This can happen only if we commit to spending a set time with the Lord each day. Making this commitment realigns our will and emotions toward new habitual paths, ordering us to freely pay attention to the beauty of God's Word and His love for us in prayer.

3. Creative Expression

Creative expression—be it artistic, mechanical, musical, or literary—also helps us to stay in communion with God. Artistic and skilled activities allow us to express the joy of being "settled" in a vocation of love and a habit of conversation with God in prayer. This expressive commitment can flow from our prayer and vocation, further securing them in our heart.

> Overseeing the mysterious laws governing the universe, the divine breath of the Creator Spirit reaches out to human genius and stirs its creative power. He touches it with a kind of inner illumination which brings together the sense of the good and the beautiful, and he awakens energies of mind and heart which enable it to conceive an idea and give it form in a work of art.[11]

The more we allow God to reach us with His love in prayer and through our fidelity to vocation, the more our minds and hearts become filled with a new energy and creativity. New ways of expressing beauty or truth, or simply expressing practical ways of getting work accomplished, will flow from our minds.

Sometimes, people feel "trapped" within their particular vocation because circumstances have overwhelmed them. Their way of life may feel constrained or routine. As our prayer life deepens, we can ask God to awaken our knowledge of our creative gifts. Enacting these gifts, as known to us in prayer and through conversation with others, can go a long way to reviving our sense of joy in living an "ordinary life." Like prayer itself, creative hobbies, pursuits, and skills break us out of our routines and give us a taste of the newness of God's own creativity. Spouses and parents should always honor creative expression, except when these activities become too consuming or are used to escape from relationships.

4. Service to Others

Similar to creative expression, service to others in need both ministers to their immediate concerns and also reminds us that our place in the world is found within a community. Service helps us transcend the self, as well as assure those who suffer that their suffering is not a sentence to loneliness and physical isolation. Just as creative expression can be a way for us to remain in reality and not slip into some dark egocentric life, so service to others also reestablishes reality by drawing us into the wounds of the human community. Such common living is the very fruit of knowing Christ sacramentally and spiritually, as His grace awakens all who know Him to notice the poor as well (Lk 10:25ff). In fact, to know Christ is to know the poor, as His own mysterious life among us was a descent into complete dependence and poverty. The reason the poor are seen as "blessed" by Christ (Lk 6:20) is because they, like Him, reveal man's true condition: all are dependent upon the providential love of God the Father.

5. Communal Worship

The central role of the Eucharist in the life and imagination of the Catholic is undeniable. For the Catholic, the Eucharist *is life*. We are called to come to Jesus in the Eucharist as we adore and praise the Father for the Son's sacrifice on the Cross, the glory of the Resurrection, and all that these loving events mean for those baptized into the Church, as well as for those who follow their conscience and seek God with a pure heart. The grace of the Holy Mass spreads throughout the world, primarily through the receptive hearts of the laity who regularly participate in worship. Within our participation in the Eucharist, the Catholic *is granted* his *deepest identity*. When we provide witness to this identity in society, the Catholic *secures* the *deepest meaning* of his relationship to Christ.

Finally, three practical tools, which will be discussed in the Appendix of this book, help secure us within the very fabric of our vocations and deepen our way of embracing renunciation and celebration: proper prayerful disposition, prayerful study of Scripture and spiritual books, and the *Consciousness Examen*.

NOTES

1.   "Sin is an offense against reason, truth, and right conscience; it is failure in genuine love for God and neighbor caused by a *perverse attachment to certain goods*. It wounds the nature of man and injures human solidarity" (emphasis mine). Sin exalts the self at the expense of truth and the good of others. See *Catechism of the Catholic Church* (Washington, DC: USCCB Publishing, 2000), sec. 1849.

2.   To have faith is to "believe in God and believe all that he has said and revealed to us . . . By faith 'man freely commits his entire self to God'" (1814). Hope is "placing our trust in Christ's promises and relying not on our own strength" (1817). To have charity is to "love God above all things for his own sake, and our neighbor as ourselves for the love of God" (1822). Charity is superior to all the virtues. For more on the virtues, see the *Catechism of the Catholic Church*, secs. 1814-1829.

3.   Wilfred Stinissen, *The Holy Spirit, Fire of Divine Love* (San Francisco: Ignatius, 2017), 21.

4.   Dom Cuthbert Butler, *Western Mysticism* (New York: Dover, 2003), 98.

5.   See 1 Kings 19:11-14.

6.   See *Catechism of the Catholic Church*, sec. 2562.

7.   Ibid., sec. 2563.

8.   See Jeremiah 20:7.

9.   See Luke 14:23.

10.   See Luke 14:17.

11.   John Paul II, *Letter to Artists* (April 4, 1999), sec. 15.

12. Paul VI, *Gaudium et Spes* (1965), sec. 24.

13. Benedict XVI, Eucharistic Celebration on the Occasion of the 23rd World Youth Day, (July 20, 2008).

14. See Luke 10:42.

Appendix

Practical Tools for Staying in Communion with God

A. Proper Prayerful Disposition: Acknowledge, Relate, Receive, Respond (ARRR)
As arranged by Jessi Kary, AO

The first tool is more a disposition for any kind of prayer rather than a prayer itself. Various moments or elements are contained within any authentic and developing prayer life, whether formal or vocal prayers, the Holy Mass, quiet adoration, or *Lectio Divina.* In all prayer, we are called to: 1) *acknowledge* our feelings, 2) *relate* them to God's loving heart, 3) *receive* what God wants to give us, and 4) *respond* in gratitude to such a gift. These are the essential elements present in any dialogue we have with God.

Acknowledge

Prayer is a relationship—a dialogue, between God and man. Because we are called to make a gift of ourselves,[1] it is necessary to first be in possession of and to know ourselves. To *acknowledge* is simply to be aware. For dialogue with God, we must specifically be aware of our thoughts, feelings, and desires, especially those that directly impact our relationship with God. What am I thinking? How do I feel? What do I desire?

Relate

Simply put, to *relate* is to tell Jesus everything! Nothing is too silly or unimportant. He already knows, but we still need to tell Him. Even if we have told Him the same thing a million times, if we find it in our hearts, we need to entrust it to Him again. Some things we take to the Father, and others seem to be matter for the Holy Spirit. Often, we speak to Jesus about our thoughts, feelings, and desires, but Mary is also constantly ready to receive all that we find in our hearts.

Receive

To *receive* simply means to be receptive to what God wants to give us. As our Holy Father Pope Emeritus Benedict XVI explains:

Prayer is pure receptivity to God's grace, love in action, communion with the Spirit who dwells within us, leading us, through Jesus, in the Church, to our heavenly Father. In the power of His Spirit, Jesus is always present in our hearts, quietly waiting for us to be still with Him, to hear His voice, to abide in His love, and to receive 'power from on high,' enabling us to be salt and light for our world.[2]

This is God's work, not ours. We must *acknowledge and relate* with the light of the Holy Spirit to dispose our heart to receive God, but it is not in our power to instigate the experience of God's love and life in our hearts. Instead, we must simply notice how our thoughts, feelings, and desires change, as well as to notice new ones. Thoughts, feelings, and desires that draw us to God, *are* God Himself.

Respond

We *respond* to gifts we receive. Our heart's natural response to God's love is gratitude. Receiving God impels us—with great ease and simplicity—to *respond*. A response flowing from the experience of God's love is accompanied by joy and is immensely fruitful, contrasting the tedious and limited results of our exertion alone, however well-intentioned we may be. In our response, we remain in the gift of God, receiving Him as we are propelled into an expression of love for our brothers and sisters. It is impossible to separate our authentic response from the action of God's love received in our heart.

Summary

To *acknowledge* the realities (thoughts, feelings, and desires) in our heart, *relate* them to the Lord, *receive* His life in us, and *respond* in gratitude and generosity with the maximum love we have received is to live the reality of our Baptism.

Nothing is too big or small to share with the infinite God who became an infant. As we converse with the Lord, we will find new experiences to bring to Him. He will heal pain and sorrow. We will know His love and His life, and He will gently lead us more deeply into His heart. From the depths of the heart of Christ into which the Father's love unceasingly gushes and the Spirit bursts forth, and into which we are drawn, new life will flow into us and flood out of us into the world, propelled in love by Love. This is reality, the one thing necessary.[3]

B. *Prayerful Study of Scripture and Spiritual Books*

The second tool is the ancient monastic experience of reading Scripture until it becomes prayer. We do this by placing ourselves in the presence of the living God and asking for His grace, which enables us to receive Him as the words we read open our hearts to Him. This is a holy exchange in which we are deeply engaged with God's love and healing. This engagement secures our own identity and mission. Knowing God without love can tyrannize the soul. *Lectio*, or *sacred reading,* is the knowledge of God in love. In such loving knowledge of God, the soul is nourished and elevated, thereby better assuring our communion with Him.

Some practical steps include:

1. Approach the text in prayerful communion. Ask the Spirit to guide and enlighten you as to content that moves you to love God. Take small portions (a sentence or two) of Scripture during this time, rather than large quantities of text.

2. Ask these questions: What does this text say? What does this text say to me? What does this text lead me to say to God? What do I detect God is saying to me through this text?

3. During or after *Lectio*, bring your contemplative insights before the Blessed Sacrament and let them rest there as your heart communes with His Sacred Heart. Christ wants to deepen your insights because He wants you to think out of what you love and to love what is

highest, Himself. The goal is to make such holy reading habitual, so that you will continue to revere both knowledge about God in Scripture and spiritual communion with God through Scripture.

4. Be aware that this knowledge is not meant for you alone. The fruit of *Lectio* is meant to be given to the Church. It is to be shared freely, but with little or no reference to the self. When done in this way, the person we share with is led to God without us getting in the way.

5. Strengthen your *Lectio* by reading spiritual books. Like Scripture, spiritual classics yield more each time we read them. Draw knowledge from these spiritual books and encounter God in prayer while reading them.

6. Go to confession often because sinful thinking patterns limit your imagination. Those with pure minds are able to delight in prayer and receive the most unthinkable callings, invitations, and consolations from God; whereas those bogged down in sin have dull vision.

7. Encourage others to holy study. By humbly inviting others into the spiritual habit of prayerful reading, you build up your family

and parish and give witness to where you "have life and have it more abundantly" (Jn 10:10).

C. Consciousness Examen

The final tool is a gift of Ignatian spirituality, the way of prayer given to the Church by St. Ignatius of Loyola. We begin this prayer by asking for light from God. We relax into God's presence. We ask for the Light to know ourselves in the Holy Spirit.

Thanksgiving

Welcome God as Gift, realizing in Him that *all is gift*.

Practical Survey of Actions

Look over the experiences of the day and the events that provoked any significant affective movement in your heart—for example, joy, pain, love, anger, anxiety, or peace. Choose an experience from the day that seems to be more significant or dominant. Ask: When or where did God especially touch my life today? When did I not allow God into my life today? In what area of my heart is God especially calling for conversion?

Sorrow and Contrition

Make some act of contrition for refusing to allow God to love you or for being too independent or too afraid to respond to His love during the day. This sorrow is hopeful; it is a recognition of your inability to respond to the Lord, while at the same time, trusting in His merciful love to begin again tomorrow.

Close by thanking God and asking for the grace to respond to His love in life-giving ways for both yourself and for those around you.

NOTES

1. Paul VI, *Gaudium et Spes* (1965), sec. 24.
2. Benedict XVI, Eucharistic Celebration on the Occasion of the 23rd World Youth Day, (July 20, 2008).
3. See Luke 10:42.